Botnet Attack Detection in the Internet of Things Using Selected Learning Algorithms

A Research Study on Securing IoT Against Cyber Threats Using Machine Learning

A Dissertation Written By

Bolakale Aremu

Botnet Attack Detection in the Internet of Things Using Selected Learning Algorithms

AB Publisher LLC

ISBN: 979-8-3492-2020-3

Published in the United States

Table of Contents

LIST OF FIGURES

LIST OF EQUATIONS

ABSTRACT

The Internet of Things (IoT) refers to a network of everyday devices, such as smartphones and industrial sensors, all connected to the Internet, allowing them to communicate and share data. IoT networks comprise various devices with different functions, communication protocols, and computational capabilities. This heterogeneity complicates the development of a one-size-fits-all solution for botnet detection. Developing effective botnet detection systems for IoT environments is challenging due to the diversity of devices, each with unique characteristics and behaviors. This study focuses on creating a robust model to identify botnet attacks across various IoT devices. Using the NB-IoT-23 datasets, which include data from five distinct devices, supervised machine learning techniques, namely Logistic Regression, Linear Regression, Artificial Neural Network (ANN), K-nearest neighbor (KNN), and Bagging, were employed to identify the most accurate and efficient method. The research highlights the Bagging ensemble technique as particularly effective. The Bagging model demonstrated remarkable performance, achieving an accuracy of 99.96%, precision of 99.93%, recall of 99.98%, an F1 score of 99.96%, and a Receiver Operating Characteristic Area Under the Curve (ROC-AUC) score of 99.96%, all within a training time of 27.59 seconds. These results suggest that the Bagging model is highly effective and very efficient, making it a strong candidate for real-world IoT botnet detection. The model's high accuracy and low computational overhead make it a viable solution for real-world applications of Botnet detection, contributing significantly to the ongoing efforts of stakeholders in securing IoT networks against botnet threats.

CHAPTER ONE

INTRODUCTION

1.1 Background to the Study

A network of internet-connected gadgets, such as smartphones, smart household appliances, industrial sensors, and medical equipment, is referred to as the Internet of Things (Adeniyi & Oyelakin, 2023). In recent years, the Internet of Things has revolutionized various industries by enabling interconnected devices to communicate and share data. However, with this increased connectivity of IoT devices, network integrity can be compromised, particularly in the form of botnet attacks (Mashaleh, Ibrahim, Alauthman, Almseidin, & Gawanmeh, 2024).

IoT device proliferation presents many benefits, but it also presents new security challenges because of the built-in constraints on processing speed, memory size, and battery life (Sai Kiran, Devisetty, Kalyan, Mukundini, & Karthi, 2020). These devices become vulnerable to targeted attacks as a result, and when botnets enter them, the consequences can be dire, ranging from network outages to illegal data access and device hijacking. This emphasizes how critical it is to identify and stop botnet attacks in IoT networks as soon as possible.

A botnet is a group of Internet of Things (IoT) that is connected to devices that attackers have infiltrated to use for illegal purposes. Botnets are networks of compromised devices that are linked together and managed by a single botmaster. Botmasters use IoT botnets to plan a variety of cyberattacks, such as denial of service (DoS) and distributed denial of service (DDoS) attacks and attempts to steal data (Farzaneh, Koosha, Boochanpour, & Alizadeh, 2020).

Botnets are becoming increasingly frequent in today's world due to their ability to spread quickly from one device to another. DDoS assaults are frequently carried out via botnets. In addition to DDoS attacks, botnets can also be used to carry out a wide variety of other malicious operations, such as spam distribution and phishing scams. However, adequate security measures, encompassing integrity, confidentiality, availability, authentication, and non-repudiation, should be essential to ensure the protection of IoT systems (Abosata, Al-Rubaye, Inalhan, & Emmanouilidis, 2021).

This study is focused on the development of a model for the detection of botnet attacks in the Internet of Things by building an effective machine learning algorithm.

1.2 Statement of the Problem

According to Thota and Menaka (2024), the wide range of IoT devices poses a major challenge for detecting botnets. These networks are made up of devices with varying functions, communication protocols, and computational capabilities. This diversity makes it difficult to design a universal solution for botnet detection. To address this, machine learning models must be trained on datasets that capture the full spectrum of devices and network behaviors present in IoT ecosystems. While obtaining such diverse data is a complex task, it is crucial for creating detection systems that can effectively adapt to and identify threats across different IoT devices (Thota & Menaka, 2024).

Furthermore, Marshan, Nizar, Ioannou and Spanaki (2023) highlighted the privacy and ethical challenges involved in using machine learning models for botnet detection in IoT networks. Machine learning algorithms typically need extensive datasets for effective training, which may include sensitive information from IoT devices. Ensuring the privacy and security of this data while still enabling effective botnet detection is a complex issue that needs to be addressed. Moreover, the deployment of these models must comply with various regulatory frameworks and ethical guidelines to prevent misuse or unintended consequences. Balancing the need for effective security measures with the protection of user privacy and compliance with regulations is a critical aspect of developing and implementing machine learning-based botnet detection systems.

An important challenge is how to choose the most effective and efficient methods for detecting botnets in the IoT network traffic. Hence, there is a need for a comparative study to be carried out.

1.3 Aim & Objectives

The aim of this study is to develop a detection model for botnet attacks in the Internet of Things (IoT) environment. The objectives are to:

(i) apply Principal Component Analysis for attribute selection;

(ii) use linear regression, logistic regression,

KNN, and ANN to classify botnet attacks in IoT;

(iii) use bagging ensemble approach to combine the strengths of each algorithm;

(iv) simulate the model in a Python environment; and

(v) evaluate the performance of the model in terms of accuracy, precision, recall, F1 Score, ROC, and time taken to build the model.

1.4 Significance of the Study

The enhanced botnet detection model will offer the potential to directly influence how security systems are designed for IoT environments, leading to more robust security protocols that can dynamically respond to new threats. It will help current research trends to ascertain the effect of some selected learning algorithms in the classification of botnet attacks.

1.5 Scope of the Study

This study focuses on the detection of botnets in the Internet of Things. Some selected machine learning algorithms; Artificial Neural Network (ANN), Linear Regression (LR), Principal Component Analysis (PCA), and K-nearest neighbourhood (KNN) were applied for the extraction of attributes. Also, an ensemble approach through the bagging method was used to build a model for detecting botnet attacks in IoT environments. Finally, a comparative study was conducted.

1.6 Definition of Operational Terms

Botnets: IoT botnets are networks of linked objects that hackers have breached to perform malicious actions.

Compromised IoT Devices: They are the primary and most crucial elements of an IoT botnet consisting of numerous linked gadgets such as televisions, thermostats, security cameras, smart home appliances, and even industrial equipment.

Command and Control (C&C) Infrastructure: The C & C infrastructure is in charge of directing the activities of the hacked devices, and serves as the main command centre for controlling the network of infected devices and distributing commands.

Exploit Kits and Malware: These are collections of software tools that include exploit codes and known vulnerabilities that can be exploited to get unauthorized access to IoT devices.

Bot Herder: The bot herder is in charge of planning and directing the entire botnet operation, which includes locating susceptible devices, setting up the infrastructure, and giving directions to carry out harmful actions.

Malicious Activities: These refer to DDoS assaults that involve employing a large number of compromised devices to overwhelm targeted networks or websites with traffic, rendering them unavailable.

Update and Maintenance Mechanisms: These are devices that bot herders use regularly to upgrade their malware, exploit kits, and botnet infrastructure.

Persistence Techniques: This entails altering the infected devices' starting scripts or services, adding covert backdoors, and changing the system settings to ensure that the botnet stays active and undiscovered even after the device is restarted or security software is installed.

Monetization: This is the development and administration of IoT botnets mainly for financial gain, such as renting botnets to other hackers or criminal groups looking to conduct DDoS attacks or other illegal operations.

Countermeasures and Prevention: This entails patching and updating IoT devices regularly to address vulnerabilities, putting robust security configurations in place, isolating IoT devices using network segmentation, and putting intrusion detection and prevention systems in place.

CHAPTER TWO

LITERATURE REVIEW

2.1 Internet of Things

The term "Internet of Things" was initially used in one of Kevin Ashton's presentations (Srivastava, Debnath, Stănică, & Pal, 2023). After initially seeming like a technological revolution, the Internet of Things is now playing a bigger role in the communication and computing industries. Over the past ten years, emerging countries have witnessed an exceptional growth rate in ICT usage, even though industrialized nations have made good progress in the ICT world for more than 20 years (Ullah & Mahmoud, 2020; Wu, Lu, Ling, Sun, & Du, 2010). IoT, which permits communication between the things in our surroundings, is responsible for the observed improvement (Luthra, Garg, Mangla, & Singh Berwal, 2018). Making the switch from traditional to intelligent corporate settings has proven to be comparatively easy for different economic sectors.

2.2 Applications of Internet of Things

Many industries have adopted IoT because it allows for the merging of virtual and real-world work experiences. These industries include supply chains, manufacturing, oil and gas, transportation, healthcare, and agriculture. According to Wahida et al. (2018), IoT is expected to have a global economic impact in the range of $3.9 to $11.1 trillion by the year 2025.

In five years, any company that slowly implements IoT

devices and technologies faces the risk of losing market share to competitors (Arnold & Voigt, 2019). This is based on Difficult Airway Society (DAS) 2023's claim that IoT-using competitors in business would be able to deliver goods and services faster and more efficiently, hence gaining market share. Consequently, implementing IoT has become crucial for competitive market performance in the current corporate environment.

2.3 Botnet Attacks

A botnet is a collection of compromised computers, also referred to as "bots," that are managed remotely by an attacker called a "botmaster" or "bot herder." Typically, software like worms or Trojan horses compromises the computers in a botnet, giving the attacker access to the compromised machines and the ability to take control of them without authorization (Pan & Yamaguchi, 2022). A computer that is a part of a botnet turns into a "bot" or "zombie" that may be controlled remotely to carry out a variety of destructive tasks. According to Winkler, Gomes and Shackleford (2017), botnets are networks of hijacked devices that are controlled by a single botmaster. They can be used to carry out a wide variety of harmful activities, including spam distribution, DDoS attacks, and phishing scams. Botnet operators may do these illicit operations on a huge scale due to the large number of infected machines, which makes it challenging for defenders to neutralize the attacks. Botnet assaults have the potential to seriously hurt people, companies, and even whole industries (Farzaneh, Koosha, Boochanpour, & Alizadeh, 2020).

In a DDoS attack, a botmaster instructs the

compromised computers to overwhelm a target website or network with traffic, rendering it unavailable to authorized users (Alaiz-Moreton et al., 2019), Botmasters can execute potent and disruptive DDoS attacks, causing large financial losses and reputational harm for the targeted businesses, by leveraging the strength of thousands or even millions of bots (Dange & Chatterjee, 2020).

According to Dange and Chatterjee (2020), compromised systems may receive commands from the botmaster instructing them to distribute spam messages that include adverts, phishing scams, or harmful links, which can then be used for several things, such as distributing malware, endorsing phoney goods, or obtaining private data from gullible people.

In credential-stuffing attacks, the botmaster uses compromised login and password combinations from data breaches and other sources to carry out botnet attacks (Farzaneh et al., 2020). This may result in unwanted access, opening the door for harmful acts like financial fraud or identity theft.

According to Alaiz-Moreton et al. (2019), botnets are also frequently used for click fraud in which automated programs mimic human clicker behaviour, thereby wasting advertiser's money and their advertising efforts.

Additionally, botnets are used to search through massive computer networks for susceptible systems to attack or compromise (Son & Mohammed, 2011). The botmaster gives the bot instructions to search IP addresses for open ports and software or services that could be susceptible (Haner & Knake, 2021). The botnet can be used to initiate targeted assaults, such as taking advantage of unpatched systems or infecting additional susceptible computers with malware, once a vulnerability has been found (Haner & Knake, 2021).

Botnets can be used by the botmaster, to mine cryptocurrencies, such as Bitcoin or Monero (Truby, 2018). As a result, the botmaster can produce virtual currency without having to pay for electricity or hardware (Wazzan, Algazzawi, Bamasaq, Albeshri, & Cheng, 2021). The victims of cryptocurrency mining botnets may experience higher electricity bills as a result of the hacked devices' severe performance degradation and increased energy consumption (Truby, 2018).

2.4 Machine Learning Algorithms

According to Sarker and Iqbal (2021), machine learning (ML) algorithms are the backbone of machine learning models. Sarker and Iqbal (2021) further explained that algorithms are sets of rules and statistical techniques that are used by computers to perform specific tasks without being explicitly programmed for those tasks. The goal of ML algorithms is for the computer to learn from the data and improve its performance. ML algorithms can be broadly categorized into three types: supervised learning, unsupervised learning, and reinforcement learning (Sarker & Iqbal, 2021).

Sarker and Iqbal (2021) explained that in supervised learning, the algorithm is trained on a labelled dataset. This means that each training example is paired with an output label. The goal is for the algorithm to learn a mapping from inputs to outputs. Examples of supervised learning are classification algorithms, such as Logistic

Regression (LR), Support Vector Machine (SVM), Decision Tree (DT) and K-Nearest Neighbours (KNN). In unsupervised learning, the algorithm is given data without explicit instructions on what to do with it. The goal is to identify patterns or structures within the data. Examples of unsupervised learning are K-Means Clustering, Hierarchical Clustering and DBSCAN (Density-Based Spatial Clustering of Applications with Noise). Sarker and Iqbal (2021) further explained that in reinforcement learning, the algorithm learns by interacting with an environment and receiving feedback in the form of rewards or penalties. The goal is to learn a strategy that maximizes cumulative rewards. Examples of reinforcement learning are Q-Learning, Deep Q-Networks (DQN) and Policy Gradient Methods.

2.5 Ensemble Learning Approach

According to Mahesh (2018), ensemble learning is a technique where multiple models are used together to tackle a computational problem. By combining multiple models, a more accurate and reliable result can be achieved. Examples of ensemble learning approaches are boosting and bagging. Bagging (Bootstrap Aggregating) involves training multiple versions of the same model on different random subsets of the training data (with replacement). The predictions of these models are then averaged (for regression) or voted on (for classification) to produce the final output. Boosting trains models sequentially, with each model trying to correct the errors of the previous ones. The final prediction is a weighted sum of the predictions from all models. Examples are AdaBoost (Adaptive Boosting), Gradient Boosting Machines (GBM), and XGBoost.

Mahesh (2018) further explained that using an ensemble learning approach offers the following benefits:

(i) **Boosting Performance**: By merging different models, the overall accuracy and effectiveness of the solution can be significantly enhanced.

(ii) **Avoiding Bad Choices**: Relying on just one model can be risky if that model is not well-suited for the task. Ensemble learning reduces this risk by spreading the decision-making across several models.

(iii) **Confidence in Decisions**: When multiple models are used to make a decision, more confidence can be obtained in the outcome. This is especially useful in critical applications like medical diagnosis.

(iv) **Feature Selection**: It can help identify which features (or variables) are most important for making accurate predictions.

(v) **Data Fusion**: Combining data from different sources can be tricky, but ensemble learning helps in integrating this information effectively.

(vi) **Incremental Learning**: Some problems require the model to learn continuously as new data arrives. Ensemble learning can adapt to these changes more smoothly.

(vii) **Non-Stationary Learning**: In environments where the underlying data patterns change over time (like stock markets), ensemble methods can adapt better to these shifts.

(viii) **Error Correction**: If one model makes a mistake, others can compensate for it. This leads to the production of more robust and reliable outcomes.

2.6 Shortcomings of the Existing Methodologies

Building on the comprehensive review of existing botnet attack detection methods presented in this chapter, there are four identified shortcomings in the existing methodologies:

(i) **Principal Component Analysis** (PCA) has not been used on large datasets with high dimensions, like IoT-23. There is a need for a balance between detection accuracy and computational efficiency using a combination of the IoT-23 dataset and PCA technique for high dimensional data analysis. This is particularly critical in the context of resource-constrained IoT devices.

(ii) **Kernel PCA**. This is an extension of PCA that allows for the application of PCA in a higher-dimensional feature space using the kernel trick. This technique is particularly useful for nonlinear dimensionality reduction, enabling the detection and projection of nonlinear relationships in data.

(iii) **Linear Discriminant Analysis** (LDA). LDA is

both a classifier and a dimensionality reduction technique. Unlike PCA, LDA attempts to model the difference between classes of data.

(iv) **T-Distributed Stochastic Neighbour Embedding** (t-SNE) is a nonlinear technique primarily used for exploring high-dimensional data and visualizing it in one, two, or three dimensions. Unlike PCA, t-SNE is a probabilistic approach that focuses on maintaining the local structure of the data, making it particularly effective for data visualization.

2.7 Related Work

Ali et al. (2024) proposed an innovative botnet identification system, ACLR, which combines artificial neural network (ANN), convolutional neural network (CNN), long short-term memory (LSTM), and recurrent neural network (RNN). Through experimentation using the UNSW-NB15 dataset, comprising nine attack types, including 'Normal', 'Generic', 'Exploits', and others, the ACLR model achieves remarkable testing accuracy (0.9698) by capturing intricate attack patterns.

Additionally, its robustness and generalizability are demonstrated through K-fold cross-validation (k = 5) with an accuracy score of 0.9749. Moreover, the proposed model exhibits high performance in botnet detection, with a receiver operating characteristic area under the curve (ROC-AUC) of 0.9934 and a precision-recall area under the curve (PR-AUC) of 0.9950.

Mishra, Paliwal and Srivastava (2024) proposed a new approach for botnet attack detection with the help of Deep Learning, specifically the Convolutional Neural Network-Pelican Optimization Algorithm (CNN-POA). The proposed approach was compared with the existing approach and other well-known algorithms for botnet attack detection with the help of the standard evaluation metrics. The simulation result shows the proposed CNN-POA as an effective and reliable method of IoT network intrusion; it outperforms a couple of other existing metaheuristic algorithms with 99.5% accuracy.

Wardana, Kołaczek, Warzyński and Sukarno (2024) introduced a novel IDS approach that employed an ensemble of traffic models from nine heterogeneous IoT devices. Using a Deep Neural Network (DNN), they created a unique training model for each device type, and combined traffic predictions from these models using ensemble averaging to enhance detection accuracy. They validated the effectiveness of this Intrusion Detection System using the N-BaIoT dataset, and demonstrated that the ensemble-averaged DNN achieves an average accuracy of 97.21%, precision of 91.41%, recall of 87.31%, and an F1-score of 88.48% in detecting botnet attacks across diverse IoT devices.

Woodiss-Field, Johnstone and Haskell-Dowland (2024) assess the applicability of established botnet detection techniques, namely, BotMiner, BotProbe, and BotHunter, on IoT-based botnets, and conducted experiments in various simulation environments created with custom network traffic generation software. The number of hosts, infection levels, types of botnet command and control (CnC), and abnormal activities are varied. Additional validation is provided by using externally sourced datasets. The findings revealed that BotMiner and BotProbe successfully identified IoT-based botnets, despite exhibiting some operational constraints.

Mishra, Paliwal and Srivastava (2024) proposed a weighted stacked ensemble model that merges deep convolutional generative adversarial networks with bidirectional long short-term memory networks. This model underwent rigorous regularization and hyperparameter optimization. Evaluation of four publicly available IoT datasets demonstrated notable enhancements in standard performance metrics for both binary and multiclass classification tasks. By leveraging L2 regularization to mitigate overfitting, the proposed model achieved a reduction in generalization error by 0.005%. Notably, the model attained an exceptional accuracy of 99.99% for BOT-IoT, 99.08% for IoT23, 99.82% for UNSWNB15, and 99.96% for ToN_IoT datasets, accompanied by improvements in Precision, Recall, and F1-score. The research presented an ensemble model comprising DCGAN and Bi-LSTM for network intrusion detection, demonstrating notable enhancements in performance metrics across various datasets.

Marshan, Nizar, Ioannou and Spanaki (2023) provided a clear overview of a study examining the use of machine learning (ML) and deep learning (DL) techniques to address the issue of online harassment by detecting the severity of abusive comments on social media, given the increasing usage of social platforms. The models employed include Naive Bayes, Random Forest, Support Vector Machine, CNN, and Bi-LSTM. The researchers also used unigrams, bigrams, and word embeddings in feature set creation. They compared multiple ML and DL models, and the specific performance metrics used, such as accuracy, precision, recall, and F1 score. They especially highlighted Random Forest as the best performer.

A study by Sharma, Mansotra and Singh (2023) underscores how the widespread deployment of IoT and Industrial IoT (IIoT) devices in previously secure areas can compromise critical infrastructure, such as intranet and database servers, due to the extensive data collection and monitoring capabilities of these devices. The paper evaluates potential security weaknesses that could lead to successful IoT attacks, highlighting prevalent Mirai botnet attack subtypes like ACK, SYN, Plain UDP, UDP flood, and Scan. Utilizing the N-BaIoT dataset, the researchers assessed the effectiveness of detection algorithms, where the CNN model demonstrated superior performance in accuracy, precision, recall, and F1-score compared to LSTM and GRU models.

Shwartz-Ziv and Armon (2022) focused on comparing the efficacy of traditional tree ensemble models, specifically XGBoost, against newer deep-learning models for handling tabular data. The methodology used is a rigorous comparison across various datasets, not only assessing performance but also considering the computational efficiency and tuning requirements of the models. The results indicated that XGBoost consistently outperforms newer deep learning models on the tested datasets, including those datasets previously used to advocate for these deep learning models. The researchers found that an ensemble of XGBoost and deep models outperform XGBoost alone.

Gandhi and Li (2021) explored how four IoT botnet datasets that were recently published, N-BaloT, IoT-23, Kitsune and MedBIoT, influenced the efficacy of 5 machine learning algorithms (Logistic regression, K-nearest neighbour, Naïve Bayes, Decision Tree, Random forest) and 2 deep learning algorithms (Multilayer Perceptron (MLPN) and Long short-term memory (LSTM)) in classifying botnet traffic. They compiled the datasets, which were all affected by the Mirai malware, from both actual and simulated IoT environments. Their findings indicated that the decision tree model not only delivered the highest accuracy but also required the least amount of time for training and testing.

Wang, Fan and Wang (2021) provided a concise overview of a comparative study between traditional machine learning and deep learning techniques for image classification, focusing on SVM (Support Vector Machine) and CNN (Convolutional Neural Network) models. By utilizing two distinct datasets-MNIST (large sample) and COREL1000 (small sample)—the study effectively demonstrated how sample size can influence the performance of these models. This approach provided different insights into the scalability and applicability of SVM and CNN under different conditions. They discovered that when using a large sample MNIST dataset, the accuracy of SVM is 0.88 while the accuracy of CNN is 0.98. However, when using a small sample COREL1000 dataset, the accuracy of SVM was found to be 0.86 while the accuracy of CNN was found to be 0.83.

Dang, Moreno-García and De la Prieta (2020) aimed to evaluate the effectiveness of deep learning models over traditional natural language processing techniques in sentiment analysis. They assessed the performance of

DNN, RNN, and CNN, utilizing Term Frequency-Inverse Document Frequency (TF-IDF) and word embeddings as feature extraction methods, and implementing these approaches on Twitter datasets. They evaluated these models based on three main metrics: overall accuracy, F-score, and processing time, offering a comprehensive overview of each model's effectiveness. They discovered that integrating deep learning methods with word embeddings yields better outcomes for sentiment analysis compared to using TF-IDF. They further demonstrated that CNNs surpassed other models in performance, achieving an optimal balance between accuracy and CPU runtime. Although RNNs display slightly greater reliability across most datasets than CNNs, they require significantly more computational time.

Ferrag, Maglaras, Moschoyiannis and Janicke (2020) utilized deep learning techniques for enhancing intrusion detection systems (IDS) in cybersecurity. The researchers presented 35 well-known cyber datasets and provided a classification of these datasets into the following 7 categories. They analyzed 7 deep learning approaches according to deep discriminative models and generative (unsupervised) models. These models were tested using two recent real traffic datasets: the CSE-CIC-IDS2018 and the Bot-IoT datasets. In the deep discriminative models, the CNN model gives the highest overall detection rate (DR Overall) with 97.28% in the CSE-CIC-IDS2018 dataset and 97.01% in the Bot-IoT dataset compared to RF, NB, SVM, and ANN. In the generative/unsupervised models, the DA model gives the highest overall detection rate (DR Overall) with 98.18% in the CSE-CIC-IDS2018 dataset and 96.84% in

Bot-IoT dataset compared to RF, NB, SVM, and ANN.

Roy et al. (2019) introduced a methodology for assessing and comparing various sets of machine learning algorithms based on specific performance metrics, including accuracy, area under the curve (AUC), and F-score. They analyzed 6 major machine learning platforms: R, Python, SAS, IBM SPSS Modeler, Microsoft Azure ML, and Apache Spark ML. The datasets used for testing came from the University of California, Irvine (UCI) library, the Kaggle competition library, and a collection of high-dimensional gene expression problems. When evaluated based on accuracy and F-score, all platforms were equally effective. However, when comparing Area Under the Curve (AUC), differences emerged, with AzureML, SAS, and Python showing superior performance. If they considered the majority of performance metrics (i.e., accuracy and F-score), it appeared that all platforms were comparably effective.

McDermott, Majdani and Petrovski (2018) introduced a sophisticated solution for identifying botnet activities within consumer IoT devices and networks. It centres on the innovative use of a Bidirectional Long Short-Term Memory (BLSTM) based Recurrent Neural Network (RNN), integrated with Word Embedding techniques to recognize texts and format data. This model enhanced traditional LSTM-RNN approaches by processing data in both forward and reverse directions, potentially capturing patterns that a unidirectional LSTM might miss. The paper provides a detailed comparative analysis between the BLSTM-RNN and traditional LSTM-RNN models. Given the increasing prevalence of IoT devices and the corresponding rise in IoT-based DDoS attacks, the study addressed a highly topical and significant issue. The development of more effective detection models is critical for enhancing the security of IoT networks.

Aral, Keskin, Kaya and Haciömeroğlu (2018) focused on utilizing advanced deep-learning architectures to improve the classification of recyclable waste. The researchers tested multiple sophisticated deep learning architectures, including DenseNet121, DenseNet169, InceptionResnetV2, MobileNet, and Xception. This variety allowed for a comprehensive evaluation of which models performed best on the TrashNet dataset, a critical factor for developing effective automated recycling solutions. They reported high-test accuracies (95% with DenseNet121 and 94% with InceptionResNetV2). These results demonstrated the efficacy of fine-tuning in deep learning models and also highlighted the potential of these technologies in real-world environmental applications.

Diro and Chilamkurti (2018) used deep learning in cybersecurity to detect attacks on the social internet of things. They tested this deep model against a traditional machine learning approach and also compared distributed attack detection to their centralized system. Their experiments showed that the distributed attack detection system outperformed centralized systems using deep learning. The researchers also demonstrated that the deep model was more effective in detecting attacks than its shallow counterparts. Furthermore, their deep learning model proved its superiority over conventional machine learning techniques like softmax in the task of classifying network data as normal or attacking previously unseen test data.

2.8 Summary of the Related Work

The summary of related work is shown in Summary 2.1.

Summary 2.1: Frame Work of Comparative Study

S/No: 1

Author(s): Ali et al., 2024

Title: Hybrid Machine Learning Model for Efficient Botnet Attack Detection in IoT Environment

Research Gap: An innovative botnet identification system, ACLR, which combined artificial neural network (ANN), convolutional neural network (CNN), long short-term memory (LSTM), and recurrent neural network (RNN).

Methodology: Model stacking is employed. It combines the outputs of various deep learning algorithms ANN, CNN, LSTM, and RNN for final prediction. Deep learning classification models are evaluated for botnet attack detection using the UNSW-NB15 dataset. Preprocessing includes handling null values and categorical data using label encoding.

Results: The ACLR model showed better performance than all other deep learning models with an accuracy score of 0.9698. ANN showed the poorest performance with an accuracy score of 0.7568.

Limitations: The ACLR model takes longer training time (4543.5s) than all other employed models.

S/No: 2

Author(s): Thota & Menaka, 2024

Title: Botnet detection in the internet-of-things networks using a convolutional neural network with a pelican optimization algorithm.

Research Gap: Addressing the problem of severely imbalanced network traffic data in the training sets used for botnet attack detection in IoT networks.

Methodology: Designing and optimizing a Convolutional Neural Network (CNN) with a Pelican Optimization Algorithm (POA) to detect botnet attacks in IoT networks.

Results: The proposed CNN-POA outperformed other existing metaheuristic algorithms (LGBA-NN, SDN, BMM and BiLSTM-CNN) with 99.5% accuracy.

Limitations: The CNN-POA model lacked scalability due to the vast data volumes from IoT sensors. It also lacks direct mechanisms for data confidentiality and security and is computationally intensive.

S/No: 3

Author(s): Wardana et al., 2024

Title: Ensemble averaging deep neural network for botnet detection in heterogeneous Internet of Things devices.

Research Gap: Detecting botnet attacks within heterogeneous IoT devices.

Methodology: Development and training of individual DNN models. After training, the prediction outputs from each device-specific DNN model were aggregated. This aggregation was done using the ensemble averaging method.

Results: The ensemble-averaged DNN achieved an average accuracy of 97.21%, precision of 91.41%, recall of 87.31%, and an F1-score of 88.48%.

Limitations: Imbalanced data management. Decentralization and scalability. Generalization and specificity of the device. Challenge of scalability.

S/No: 4

Author(s): Woodiss-Field et al., 2024

Title: Examination of Traditional Botnet Detection on IoT-Based Bots.

Research Gap: Assessing the applicability of established botnet detection techniques, namely, BotMiner, BotProbe, and BotHunter, on IoT-based botnets.

Methodology: Conducted experiments in various simulation environments created with custom network traffic generation software.

Results: BotMiner and BotProbe successfully identified IoT-based botnets. Research demonstrated that traditional botnet detection methods could effectively recognize botnets in IoT contexts, with different techniques potentially offering complementary strengths.

Limitations: Technique-specific constraints: BotHunter was unable to detect bots in both traditional and IoT scenarios. Protocol Dependency: The detection techniques proved more effective with botnets utilizing the IRC protocol, particularly BotProbe.

S/No: 5

Author(s): Mishra, Paliwal and Srivastava (2024)

Title: Anomaly detection using deep convolutional generative adversarial networks in the internet of things.

Research Gap: A weighted stacked ensemble model that merges deep convolutional generative adversarial networks with Bi-LSTM networks.

Methodology: Employing an ensemble of neural networks for intrusion detection, utilizing datasets BOT-IoT, IoT-23, UNSWNB15, and ToN-IoT. BOT-IoT dataset This dataset captured various types of attacks for real-time analysis within the proposed framework.

Results: The model achieved a reduction in generalization error by 0.005%. It attained an exceptional accuracy of 99.99% for BOT-IoT, 99.08% for IoT23, 99.82% for UNSWNB15, and 99.96% for ToN_IoT datasets, accompanied by improvements in Precision, Recall, and F1-score.

Limitations: Hyperparameter tuning and data management remain unresolved. IoT networks' privacy and security concerns persist due to the vast amount of real-time data they generate.

S/No: 6

Author(s): Marshan, Nizar, Ioannou and Spanaki (2023)

Title: Comparing Machine Learning and Deep Learning

Techniques for Text Analytics: Detecting the Severity of Hate Comments Online.

Research Gap: Detection of the severity of abusive comments using machine learning (ML) and deep learning (DL) models.

Methodology: ML and DL models including Naive Bayes, Random Forest, SVM, CNN, and Bi-LSTM were used to detect the severity of abusive comments on social media. Feature sets were created using unigrams, bigrams, and word embeddings.

Results: Performance metrics like accuracy, precision, recall, and F1 score were compared. Random Forest performed best.

Limitations: Limited generalizability due to publicly available datasets. Small dataset size hampers advanced embedding techniques. Manual word embedding was performed, which might not capture the nuances and complexities of language as effectively as pre-trained embeddings. Lack of comparison with deep learning models. Absence of context analysis for previous posts.

S/No: 7

Author(s): Sharma et al., 2023

Title: Detection of Mirai Botnet Attacks on IoT devices Using Deep Learning.

Research Gap: Evaluation of potential security weaknesses that could lead to successful IoT attacks, highlighting prevalent Mirai botnet attack subtypes like

ACK, SYN, Plain UDP, UDP flood, and Scan.

Methodology: A comparative analysis of different deep learning models (CNNs, LSTM and Gated Recurrent Unit networks (GRUs)) to detect botnet attacks on IoT devices using the N-BaIoT dataset.

Results: CNN model demonstrated superior performance in accuracy, precision, recall, and F1-score compared to LSTM and GRU models.

Limitations: The study was limited by its reliance on the N-BaIoT dataset which did not encompass the full range of IoT botnet behaviours and lacked diversity in attack types. Furthermore, the models tested, particularly CNNs, although effective, still faced challenges with real-time data processing and generalization across varied IoT environments.

S/No: 8

Author(s): Chwartz-ziv and Armon (2022)

Title: Tabular Data: Deep Learning is not All you Need.

Research Gap: Comparison of the efficacy of traditional tree ensemble models, specifically XGBoost, against newer deep learning models for handling tabular data.

Methodology: A comparison of model performance across multiple datasets, focusing on both computational efficiency and tuning needs.

Results: Findings revealed that XGBoost outperformed newer deep learning models, even on the researchers' advocated datasets, and suggested a hybrid approach with XGBoost and deep models as the most effective.

Limitations: Despite significant progress, deep models did not outperform XGBoost in the explored datasets, indicating a need for further research. Future studies should systematically evaluate performance on diverse datasets and consider improving model optimization to compete with XGBoost's ease of hyperparameter tuning.

S/No: 9

Author(s): Gandhi and Li (2021)

Title: Comparing Machine Learning and Deep Learning for IoT Botnet Detection.

Research Gap: Investigation of how 4 recently published IoT botnet datasets, N-BaIoT, IoT-23, Kitsune and MedBIoT, influence the efficacy of 5 machine learning and 2 deep learning algorithms in classifying botnet traffic.

Methodology: 4 datasets, N-BaIoT, IoT-23, Kitsune, and MedBIoT were derived from both actual and simulated IoT environments impacted by the Mirai malware, providing a rich basis for analysis across different scenarios and conditions. The researchers selected 5 ML algorithms (Logistic Regression, KNN, Naïve Bayes, Decision Tree, Random Forest) and 2 DL algorithms (MLP and LSTM)) to analyze the botnet traffic data.

Results: The decision Tree model emerged as the most effective, achieving the highest accuracy and requiring the least amount of time for training and testing.

Limitations: The research relied on existing datasets for comparison studies of machine learning algorithms. This did not fully address specific challenges. Future work aimed to overcome these limitations by collecting a tailored dataset. There remained ample opportunity for further refinement and exploration of additional machine learning algorithms to enhance detection efficiency.

S/No: 10

Author(s): Wang, Fan and Wang (2021)

Title: Comparative Analysis of Image Classification Algorithms Based on Traditional Machine Learning and Deep Learning.

Research Gap: Provision of a good understanding of how dataset size affects the performance of SVM and CNN models.

Methodology: Rigorous assessment and comparison of the scalability and applicability of SVM and CNN models concerning dataset size. This structured approach allowed for a clear understanding of how each model's performance varied with changes in data volume and complexity, providing valuable guidance in selecting the most appropriate model for specific needs in image classification.

Results: When the researchers used a large MNIST dataset, the SVM achieved an accuracy of 0.88 compared to CNN's 0.98. However, with a smaller COREL1000 dataset, the SVM's accuracy was 0.86.while the accuracy of CNN was found to be 0.83. Therefore, SVM performed better with smaller datasets while CNN excelled in larger datasets.

Limitations: Generalizability: Findings might not apply

to other datasets or real-world scenarios.

Evaluation Metrics: Sole reliance on accuracy might not provide a complete assessment of performance.

S/No: 11

Author(s): Dang, Moreno-García and De la Prieta (2020)

Title: Sentiment Analysis Based on Deep Learning: A Comparative Study.

Research Gap: Evaluation of the effectiveness of deep learning models over traditional natural language processing techniques in sentiment analysis.

Methodology: Evaluation of the performance of DNN, RNN, and CNN, incorporating feature extraction techniques like Term Frequency-Inverse Document Frequency (TF-IDF) and word embeddings, applying these models to Twitter datasets. The experiment compared these models using three primary metrics: overall accuracy, F-score, and processing time, providing a holistic view of each model's performance.

Results: The study found that using word embedding alongside deep learning techniques was more effective than combining them with TF-IDF for sentiment analysis. Additionally, the experiments showed that CNN performed better than other models, offering a good trade-off between accuracy and CPU runtime. While RNN had slightly higher reliability than CNN with most datasets, its computational time was significantly longer.

Limitations: The computational time of RNN was much

longer than that of CNN. Although different deep learning models like CNN, RNN, and LSTM were tested individually, the paper lacked comparative analysis across the three models.

S/No: 12

Author(s): Ferrag, Maglaras, Moschoyiannis and Janicke (2020)

Title: Deep Learning For Cyber Security Intrusion Detection: Approaches, Datasets, and Comparative Study.

Research Gap: Utilization of deep learning techniques for enhancing intrusion detection systems (IDS) in cybersecurity. The study addressed the protection of Critical National Infrastructures (CNIs) and the use of Supervisory Control and Data Acquisition (SCADA) systems, which were vital for operational integrity in various sectors.

Methodology: The researchers presented 35 well-known cyber datasets and provided a classification of these datasets into 7 categories: (i) network traffic-based dataset, (ii) electrical network-based dataset, (iii) internet traffic-based dataset, (iv) virtual private network-based dataset, (v) android apps-based dataset, (vi) IoT traffic-based dataset, and (vii) internet-connected devices-based dataset. These models were tested using two recent real traffic datasets: the CSE-CIC-IDS2018 and the Bot-IoT datasets.

Results: The research compared the performance of 7 deep learning approaches with 4 machine learning approaches, such as NB, ANN, SVM, and RF, based on the global detection rate (DR Overall). Among the deep discriminative models, the CNN model achieved the highest DR Overall, reaching 97.28% in the CSE-CIC-IDS2018 dataset and 97.01% in the Bot-IoT dataset, surpassing RF, NB, SVM, and ANN. In contrast, among the generative/unsupervised models, the DA model achieved the highest DR Overall, with 98.18% in the CSE-CIC-IDS2018 dataset and 96.84% in the Bot-IoT dataset, also outperforming RF, NB, SVM, and ANN.

Limitations: The classification and analysis are based on a selected number of datasets which do not fully represent all potential scenarios in cybersecurity. This specificity limits the generalizability of the findings across different environments and attack vectors. Model comparison: While the methodology includes a comparison between deep learning and traditional machine learning models, the effectiveness of these comparisons is limited because the datasets used do not fully test the range of capabilities of each model.

The depth of comparison is constrained by the diversity and complexity of the datasets.

S/No: 13

Author(s): Roy et al. (2019)

Title: Performance Comparison of Machine Learning Platforms.

Research Gap: A well-defined approach for comparing machine learning platforms, utilizing various common algorithms and metrics (accuracy, F-score, and AUC). This comparative analysis aimed to identify platforms that performed best on specific metrics.

Methodology: The study compared 6 popular ML platforms (R, Python, SAS, IBM SPSS Modeler, Microsoft Azure ML, and Apache Spark ML) for classification tasks. They tested each platform with 6 classification algorithms (SVM, MLP, RF and variants, decision trees and gradient boosted trees, NB and Bayesian networks, and logistic regression) using metrics like accuracy, F-score, and AUC. The data for testing came from the UCI library, Kaggle, and high-dimensional gene expression problems, with hyperparameter tuning performed where applicable.

Results: When evaluated based on accuracy and F-score, all platforms were equally effective, even though some platforms had restricted or no options for parameter tuning. However, when comparing Area Under the Curve (AUC), differences emerged, with AzureML, SAS and Python showing superior performance. If the researchers considered the majority of performance metrics (i.e., accuracy and F-score), it appeared that all platforms are comparably effective.

Limitations: Focus on specific performance metrics: The study emphasized traditional performance measures like accuracy, F-score, and AUC. While these are common metrics, they may not fully capture all relevant aspects of performance, such as computational efficiency, scalability, or the handling of imbalanced data. Comparative analysis: The method for comparing the platforms may not account for all factors that influence the practical deployment of machine learning solutions, such as user interface, ease of integration into existing workflows, cost, and support.

S/No: 14

Author(s): McDermott, Majdani and Petrovski (2018)

Title: Botnet Detection in the Internet of Things using Deep Learning Approaches.

Research Gap: A sophisticated solution for identifying botnet activities within consumer IoT devices and networks.

Methodology: Innovative use of a Bidirectional Long Short-Term Memory (BLSTM) based Recurrent Neural Network (RNN), integrated with Word Embedding techniques for text recognition and data formatting, This was an application of a BLSTM-RNN model to detect botnet activities. This model enhances traditional LSTM-RNN approaches by processing data in both forward and reverse directions, potentially capturing patterns that a unidirectional LSTM might miss.

Results: The bidirectional approach of the BLSTM-RNN offers improved detection capabilities, given the increasing prevalence of IoT devices and the corresponding rise in IoT-based DDoS attacks. The development of more effective detection models was critical for enhancing the security of IoT networks.

Limitations: Dataset Constraints: The study was limited to specific attack vectors of the Mirai botnet and might not generalize to other botnet types or broader IoT threats.

Sample Size: Insufficient sample sizes for certain attack types may have hindered model accuracy and loss metrics, particularly for the 'ack' attack vector.

Computational Overhead: The bidirectional LSTM

approach, while effective, significantly increases processing time, potentially limiting its applicability in real-time detection scenarios.

Focus on Specific Features: The detection strategy is focused on packet-level features, which may not capture all types of botnet behaviors.

S/No: 15

Author(s): Aral, Keskin, Kaya and Haciömeroğlu (2018)

Title: Classification of TrashNet Dataset Based on Deep Learning Models.

Research Gap: Utilization of advanced deep learning architectures to improve the classification of recyclable waste.

Methodology: The researchers tested multiple deep learning architectures, including DenseNet121, DenseNet169, InceptionResnetV2, MobileNet, and Xception. This variety allowed for a comprehensive evaluation of which models perform best on the TrashNet dataset. The use of different optimizers (Adam and Adadelta) and data augmentation due to limited sample sizes indicated a methodologically sound approach.

Results: The reported high-test accuracies (95% with DenseNet121 and 94% with InceptionResNetV2) were impressive. These results not only demonstrated the efficacy of fine-tuning in deep learning models but also highlighted the potential of these technologies in real-world environmental applications.

Limitations: The study was limited by its use of the Trashnet dataset, which had insufficient samples, potentially affecting the generalizability of the findings. Also, the research only compared a few deep learning architectures and two optimizers, limiting the exploration of possibly more effective models and optimization strategies.

S/No: 16

Author(s): Diro and Chilamkurti (2018)

Title: Distributed Attack Detection Scheme Using Deep Learning Approach for Internet Of Things.

Research Gap: Adoption of deep learning approach to cybersecurity for detecting attacks in social internet of things.

Methodology: The researchers compared how well a DL model performed against the traditional ML approach. In addition, they assessed the effectiveness of distributed attack detection compared to their centralized detection system.

Results: Their distributed attack detection system outperformed centralized systems using a DL model. The deep model was more effective in detecting attacks than its shallow counterparts, showing its superiority over conventional ML techniques.

Limitations: The system's effectiveness was not tested across diverse datasets and against a broad range of machine-learning algorithms. Also, it does not utilize network payload data, which might contain essential discriminatory features for attack detection.

2.9 Research Gap

The comprehensive review of botnet detection methods highlights a critical gap in existing approaches, particularly in the context of high-dimensional IoT datasets like NB-IoT-23. While Principal Component Analysis (PCA) is a well-established technique for dimensionality reduction, its application to large-scale, high-dimensional datasets such as IoT-23 remains underexplored. This gap is significant given the pressing need to balance detection accuracy with computational efficiency in resource-constrained IoT environments.

To address this gap, this research uses a novel approach combining PCA for feature selection with five learning algorithms for a robust detection of botnet attack. This approach aims to reduce the high dimensionality of NB-IoT-23 network data, improving computational efficiency while maintaining robust detection capabilities.

CHAPTER THREE

METHODOLOGY

3.1 Introduction

This chapter discusses the approach to achieve all the goals stated in the first chapter, every step in the methodology is explained in this chapter clearly and logically to match the activities required to achieve each research objective of the study.

3.2 Developed Botnet Detection Model

The approach to actualization of the study is given a stepwise method. Data acquisition was achieved through a publicly available dataset. The IoT botnet datasets were loaded, balancing the data using the Synthetic Minority Oversampling Technique (SMOTE), reducing the dimensionality of the attributes with PCA, and training the model with LR, KNN, ANN), and also the ensemble classifiers by bagging. Figure 3.1 shows the framework of the developed botnet detection model.

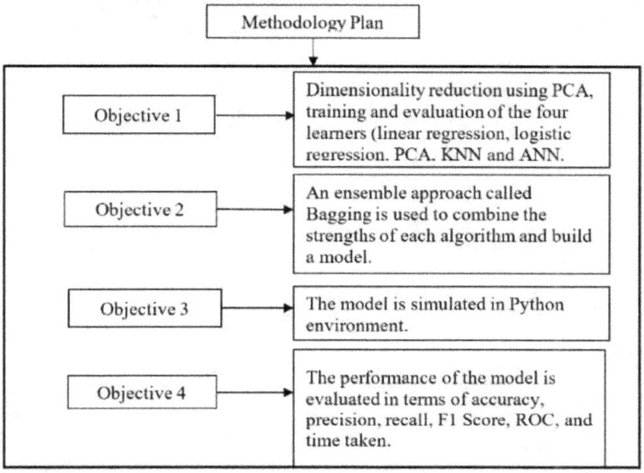

Figure 3.1: Framework of the Botnet Detection Model

3.3 Data Acquisition

Recent and comprehensive, high-dimensionality datasets that include both normal traffic and botnet traffic from IoT environments are gathered. Recent NB-IoT-23 datasets are gathered from the Kaggle repository, a publicly available source, (Meidan et al., 2018). Dataset Link: https://www.kaggle.com/datasets/saurabhshahane/anomaly-detection-using-deep-learning?resource=download. A sample of the *Mirai_danmini_doorbell_test* dataset is shown in Figure 3.2.

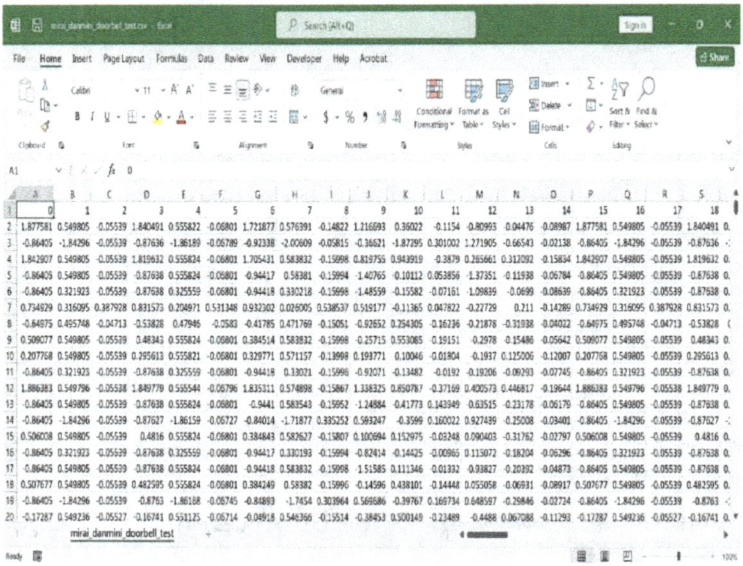

Figure 3.2: Mirai_danmini_doorbell_test data from NB-IoT-23 dataset (Meidan et al., 2018)

The dataset has been specifically pre-processed by Meidan et al. (2018). The NB-IoT-23 datasets were collected from five distinct IoT devices which are listed as follows:

- i. Danmini doorbell (4 datasets)
- ii. Ecobee thermostat (4 datasets)
- iii. Philips baby monitor (4 datasets)
- iv. Provision security camera (4 datasets)
- v. Samsung webcam (2 datasets)

The total number of datasets is 18 (9 training sets and 9 testing sets). The datasets include various IoT devices targeted by Gafgyt and Mirai botnets.

3.4 Data Pre-processing

Using Jupyter Notebook and Python, the multiple CSV files containing the datasets files are loaded in Jupyter and then combined into a single DataFrame using pandas. The file paths for training and testing datasets are specified for both Gafgyt and Mirai botnets targeting different IoT devices. The training and testing datasets are loaded using the *load_data* function.

3.4.1 Handling Class Imbalance

Balancing Data with SMOTE: Synthetic Minority Over-sampling Technique (SMOTE) is applied to balance the training dataset. Dimensionality reduction with PCA: Principal Component Analysis (PCA) is used to reduce the number of features to 30 to handle high-dimensional data effectively.

3.4.2 Algorithm of the PCA

Step 1: Standardize the Data.

Center the data by subtracting the mean of each feature from the dataset. This ensures that each feature has a mean of zero. Scale the data so that each feature has a unit variance. This is particularly important when features are measured on different scales.

$$X_{scaled} = \frac{X - \mu}{\delta}, \qquad (3.1)$$

Where μ is the mean of each feature and σ is the standard deviation.

Step 2: Compute the Covariance Matrix

Calculate the covariance matrix to understand how the variables relate to each other.

$$\text{Cov(X)} = \frac{1}{n-1} X_{scaled}^{T} X_{scaled} , \tag{3.2}$$

where X_{scaled} is the standardized data matrix and n is the number of observations.

Step 3: Compute the Eigenvalues and Eigenvectors.

Calculate the eigenvalues and eigenvectors of the covariance matrix. Eigenvalues indicate the amount of variance carried by each principal component, while eigenvectors define the direction of these components.

$$\text{Cov(X)}v = \lambda v, \tag{3.3}$$

where λ are the eigenvalues and v are the corresponding eigenvectors.

Step 4: Sort Eigenvalues and Eigenvectors

Sort the eigenvalues in descending order. The eigenvector corresponding to the largest eigenvalue is the first principal component, the one with the second largest is the second principal component, and so on.

Step 5: Select Principal Components

Choose the top *k* eigenvectors (principal components) that correspond to the *k* largest eigenvalues. This selection determines the reduced dimensionality of the dataset.

Step 6. Transform the Data:

Project the original data onto the k-selected principal

components to obtain the new k-dimensional feature space.

$$X_{reduced} = X_{scaled} \cdot W \qquad (3.4)$$

where W is a matrix of the top k eigenvectors.

Train-Validation Split: The resampled training data is split into training and validation sets to evaluate model performance during training.

3.4.3 Train-Validation Split

The resampled training data is split into training and validation sets to evaluate model performance during training. The dataset is now divided into two parts: 80% is used for training, and 20% is used for testing. This separation is crucial because it ensures that each time a machine learning model is trained, it is evaluated on new or unseen data. The training set, which makes up 80% of the data, is used to teach the model the relationships and patterns within the dataset. The test set, which comprises the remaining 20%, is used to assess how well the model performs on data it has never encountered before.

This process helps to verify that the model does not overfit the training data. Overfitting occurs when the model learns the training data too well, including its noise and outliers, and as a result, fails to perform effectively on new or unseen data. Using a separate test set ensures that the model generalizes well and provides accurate predictions on new observations. The ratio of 20% to 80% was used to ensure that the model is very robust.

3.5 Development Environment of the Model

To train the supervised machine learning models using Python in Jupyter Notebook the following steps are taken:

(i) Metrics Dictionary: A dictionary is initialized to store evaluation metrics for each model.

(ii) ROC Curve Plotting: A function is defined to plot the Receiver Operating Characteristic (ROC) curve for model evaluation.

(iii) Logistic Regression: Logistic Regression is trained, and its performance is evaluated on the validation set. Metrics such as accuracy, precision, recall, F1 score, and ROC AUC are computed.

(iv) Linear Regression: Linear Regression is used for classification by treating predicted values greater than 0.5 as class 1 and others as class 0. The model is evaluated similarly to Logistic Regression.

(v) K-Nearest Neighbors (KNN): The KNN model is trained and evaluated on the validation set, with metrics recorded.

(vi) Artificial Neural Network (ANN): An ANN is trained using the MLP Classifier. Its performance is evaluated, and metrics are recorded.

(vii) Bagging Classifier: A Bagging Classifier, which uses a base estimator and fits multiple versions of the model on random subsets of the dataset, is trained. The model's performance is evaluated on the validation set, and metrics are recorded.

The predictions of the learners are aggregated by using the bagging ensemble method. The ensemble approach used is illustrated in Figure 3.3.

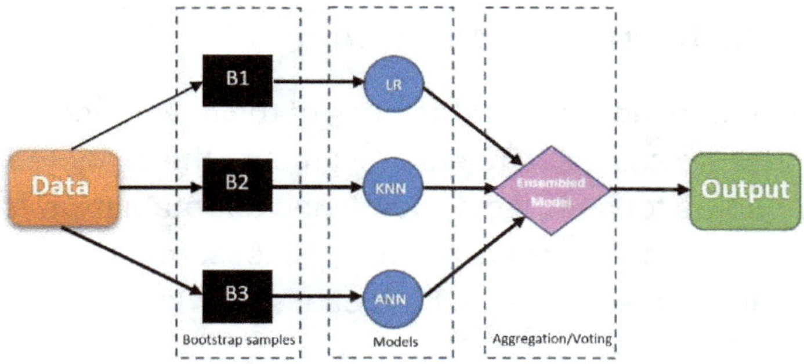

Figure 3.3: An illustration of Bagging Ensemble Approach

3.6 Bagging Ensemble Method

Bagging, an acronym for bootstrap aggregating, is an ensemble technique that is used to train multiple models (LR, KNN and ANN) independently using randomly selected subsets of the dataset. Their predictions are then combined through voting or averaging. Specifically, each model is trained on a bootstrap sample, a random subset of the data (B1, B2 or B3) created by sampling with replacement, allowing individual data points to appear multiple times in the subset. This process ensures that each model sees a different portion of the dataset, which helps reduce variance.

By averaging the predictions from these independently trained models, the final aggregated model captures the strengths of each while mitigating their individual errors. This makes bagging an effective approach to reduce overfitting and improve robustness, particularly for models that are highly variable.

3.7 Performance Evaluation

The effectiveness and efficiency of the developed model are assessed to ensure it meets the expected standards for accuracy, speed, and adaptability in real-world scenarios, using the model assessment metrics explained in section 3.7.1 (Ali et al., 2024):

3.7.1 Accuracy

It measures the proportion of total correct predictions (both true positives and true negatives) out of all predictions made. It can be calculated from equation (3.5).

$$\text{Accuracy} = \frac{(\text{TP+TN})}{(\text{TP+TN+FP+FN})} \quad (3.5)$$

TP = True Positive, TN = True Negative, FP = False Positive, FN = False Negative

3.7.2 Precision

It assesses the accuracy of positive predictions and can be calculated from equation (3.6).

$$\text{Precision} = \frac{\text{TP}}{(\text{TP+FP})} \quad (3.6)$$

3.7.3 Recall (Sensitivity)

It indicates the ability of the model to detect all actual positives, measuring the percentage of true positives identified correctly. It can be calculated from equation 3.7.

$$\text{Recall} = \frac{\text{TP}}{(\text{TP+FN})} \tag{3.7}$$

3.7.4 F1-Score

It is the harmonic mean of precision and recall. It provides a balance between the two in cases where an equilibrium is needed for effective performance evaluation. It can be calculated from equation (3.8).

$$\text{F1-Score} = \frac{2(\text{Precision} \times \text{Recall})}{(\text{Precision+Recall})} \tag{3.8}$$

3.7.5 ROC

This metric evaluates the ability of the model to discriminate between the classes at various threshold settings. It can also be written as ROC-AUC or AUC-ROC and can be obtained from equation (3.9).

$$\text{ROC-AUC} = \int_0^1 TPR(FPR)dFPR \tag{3.9}$$

TPR = True Positive Rate (Recall)

FPR = False Positive Rate, and can be calculated from equation (3.10).

$$\text{FPR} = \frac{\text{FP}}{(\text{FP+TN})} \tag{3.10}$$

CHAPTER FOUR

RESULTS AND DISCUSSION

4.1 Experimental Analysis

To efficiently detect botnet attacks, Jupyter Lab is used because it offers greater control over the local environment. Unlike Google Colaboratory, there are no usage limits. In addition, there is enhanced privacy and security. Jupyter Lab allows offline access, seamless integration with local tools and resources, and full utilization of system hardware. A core i5 system was used in this experiment. The following machine learning models were trained and evaluated on the NB-IoT-23 datasets: Linear Regression, Logistic Regression, K-nearest neighbors (KNN), Artificial Neural Networks (ANN), and Bagging Classifier. The datasets include various IoT devices targeted by two botnets called Gafgyt and Mirai. The latest Python version 3.12.4 was installed in the system. The following libraries are also installed: pandas, sci-kit-learn, imbalanced-learn, matplotlib, and numpy.

4.2 Results of Loading and Pre-processing of Dataset

Loading CSV Files: The *load_data* function reads multiple CSV files into a single pandas DataFrame.

Defining File Paths: File paths for training and testing datasets are specified for both Gafgyt and Mirai botnets targeting different IoT devices.

Loading Data: Training and testing data are loaded using the *load_data* function.

Handling Class Imbalance: If the training data has only one class, it is combined with the testing data to ensure both classes are represented. The combined data was then split into training and testing sets.

Balancing Data with SMOTE: Synthetic Minority Over-sampling Technique (SMOTE) was applied to balance the training dataset.

Dimensionality Reduction with PCA: Principal Component Analysis (PCA) reduces the number of features to 30 to handle high-dimensional data effectively.

Train-validation Split: The resampled training data was split into training and validation sets to evaluate model performance during training.

4.3 Training of Model and Evaluation Process

Metrics dictionary: A dictionary was initialized to store evaluation metrics for each model.

ROC Curve Plotting: A function was defined to plot the Receiver Operating Characteristic (ROC) curve for model evaluation.

Linear Regression: Linear Regression was used for classification by treating predicted values greater than 0.5 as class 1 and others as class 0. The performance of the model was evaluated on the validation set. Metrics such as accuracy, precision, recall, F1 score, and ROC AUC were computed.

Logistic Regression: Logistic Regression was trained, and its performance was evaluated similarly to Linear Regression.

K-Nearest Neighbors (KNN): The KNN model was trained using the *KNeighborsClassifier*

and evaluated on the validation set with metrics recorded.

Artificial Neural Network (ANN): An ANN was trained using the *MLPClassifier*. Its performance was evaluated and metrics were recorded.

Bagging Classifier: A Bagging classifier, which uses a base estimator and fits multiple versions of the model on random subsets of the dataset, was trained. The model's performance was evaluated on the validation set, and metrics were recorded.

4.3.1 Creating and Training the Bagging (Voting) Classifier

The voting classifier, which is the ensemble model used in this research, was created using Logistic Regression, KNN, ANN, and the custom Linear Regression classifier. Each learner was wrapped in a pipeline with *StandardScaler* to standardize the data before fitting. This standardization ensures that features were scaled to a uniform range, which is crucial for the effective performance of algorithms sensitive to feature magnitudes. The model employed both soft and hard voting strategies, allowing for flexibility in aggregating predictions. Additionally, hyperparameter tuning was performed for each base learner to optimize their performance, ensuring the ensemble model's robustness and improved accuracy in botnet attack detection.

4.3.2 Results of Comparison Using Styled DataFrame

Finally, results were compared in a table using a styled data frame. This is a table that compares the training times of all the learners and the voting classifier was plotted.

4.4 Results of the Botnet Detection Model

The results of the developed botnet detection model are based in terms of accuracy, precision, recall, F1-score, ROC-AUC and training time or time taken to build the model given in the following subsections:

4.4.1 Result of Linear Regression Classifier

The result of the linear regression classifier is shown in Table 4.1.

Table 4.1: Evaluation Metrics for Linear Regression

Learning Algorithm	Evaluation Metrics					
	Accuracy	Precision	Recall	F1 Score	ROC-AUC	Training Time (s)
Linear Regression	0.9132	0.9939	0.8316	0.9061	0.9934	0.43

In Table 4.1, the comparison of the effectiveness of various metrics on linear regression was carried out. The evaluation metrics based on Linear Regression demonstrate strong performance. This learner achieved an accuracy of 91.32%, indicating its overall effectiveness in correctly classifying botnet attacks within the dataset. The precision of 99.39% highlights its exceptional ability to correctly identify positive cases, minimizing false positives. However, the recall, which measures the model's capacity to detect all actual positive cases, is slightly lower at 83.16%, suggesting that some true positives may have been missed. The F1-score, which balances precision and recall, is a robust 90.61%, reflecting a well-rounded performance in detecting botnet activities.

Furthermore, the ROC-AUC score of 0.9934 underscores the learner's excellent ability to distinguish between positive and negative cases. The training time of only 0.43 seconds demonstrates the computational efficiency of the Linear Regression algorithm, making it highly suitable for resource-constrained IoT environments. These results indicate that the model effectively balances precision and computational efficiency, though slight improvements in recall could further enhance its detection capabilities.

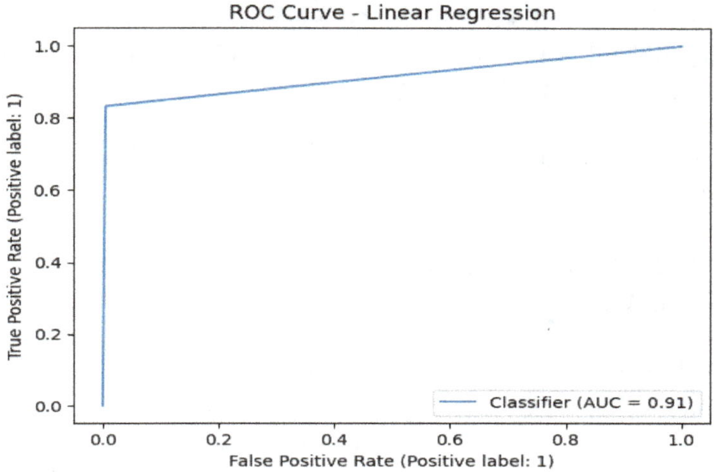

Figure 4.1: ROC-AUC curve for linear regression

The ROC curve for the Linear Regression classifier, as displayed in Figure 4.1, provides valuable insight into the model's classification performance. The curve shows the trade-off between the True Positive Rate (TPR) and False Positive Rate (FPR) across different classification thresholds. The steep initial rise in the curve indicates that the classifier is capable of achieving a high TPR with a minimal FPR at lower thresholds. This reflects the classifier's strong ability to correctly identify true positives while avoiding false positives.

The area under the curve (AUC) is 0.91, which confirms excellent discrimination capability of the model. A high AUC value indicates that the Linear Regression classifier is effective in distinguishing between the positive (botnet) and negative (non-botnet) classes. While the curve does not perfectly reach the top-left corner, which represents an ideal classifier, the classifier's performance is robust and reliable. The graph validates the earlier numerical ROC-AUC score (0.9934), suggesting that the classifier performs well across varying threshold settings.

4.4.2 Result of the Logistic Regression Classifier

The result of the logistic regression classifier is shown in Figure 4.2.

Table 4.2: Evaluation Metrics for Logistic Regression

Learning Algorithm	Evaluation Metrics					
	Accuracy	Precision	Recall	F1 Score	ROC-AUC	Training Time (s)
Logistic Regression	0.9944	0.9977	0.8316	0.9910	0.9943	3.34

The performances of various metrics on logistic regression as shown in Table 4.2. The evaluation metrics using Logistic Regression indicate exceptional overall performance. The model achieved an accuracy of 99.44%, reflecting its effectiveness in correctly classifying the majority of instances. A precision of 99.77% highlights its strong capability to correctly identify positive cases with minimal false positives.

Similar to the Linear Regression, the recall remains at 83.16%, indicating room for improvement in detecting all true positives. However, the F1-score, which balances precision and recall, is remarkably high at 99.10%, showcasing the model's ability to handle the trade-off effectively.

The ROC-AUC score of 0.9943 further reinforces the classifier's outstanding classification capabilities, demonstrating its ability to distinguish between positive and negative cases across various thresholds. However, the training time for Logistic Regression is significantly longer at 3.34 seconds compared to Linear Regression, which may pose a limitation in time-sensitive or resource-constrained IoT environments. Despite this, the Logistic Regression classifier's high precision and accuracy make it a robust choice for botnet detection, provided that computational resources are sufficient to handle its longer training time.

The ROC-Curve is shown in Figure 4.2

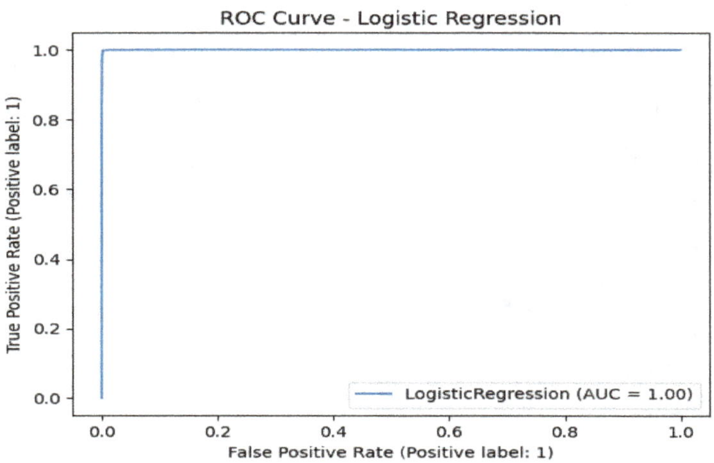

Figure 4.2: ROC-AUC Curve for Logistic Regression

4.4.3 Result of the KNN Classifier

The result of K-nearest Neighbor used in evaluation metrics is shown in Table 4.3

Table 4.3: Evaluation Metrics for KNN

Learning Algorithm	Evaluation Metrics					
	Accuracy	Precision	Recall	F1 Score	ROC-AUC	Training Time (s)
KNN	1.0000	1.0000	1.0000	1.0000	1.0000	0.13

The performances of various metrics on KNN as shown in Table 4.3, all the metrics recorded the highest performance of 1.0000. The lowest training time of 0.13s was achieved too indicating high computational efficiency.

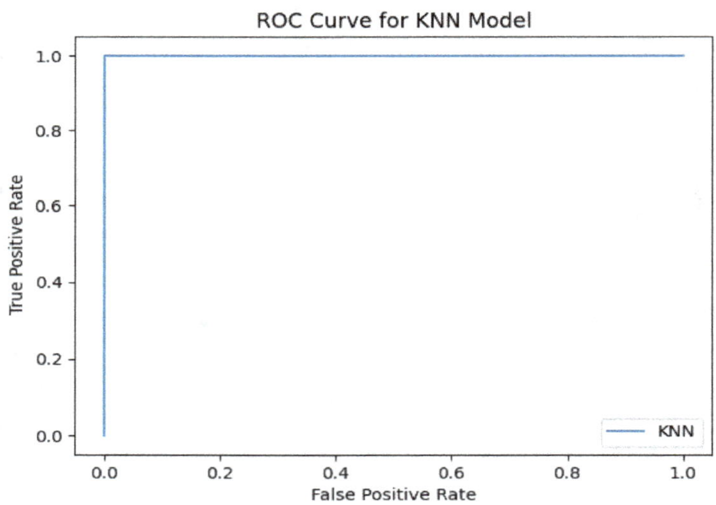

Figure 4.3: ROC-AUC curve for KNN

The ROC curve shown for the KNN classifier is highly indicative of a strong classification performance. The curve immediately rises to the top-left corner (True

Positive Rate of 1.0 and False Positive Rate of 0.0), suggesting that the model achieves perfect classification without any trade-off between sensitivity and specificity. The Area Under the ROC Curve (AUC) is very close to 1.0, which indicates excellent model performance. The KNN model performs flawlessly, with no false positives or false negatives during testing.

This could be an indication that the model is either very well-trained or that the dataset might have characteristics that make it easy to separate classes (e.g., the classes are highly distinct or well-defined).

4.4.4 Result of ANN Classifier

The result of ANN used in evaluation metrics is shown in Table 4.3

Table 4.4: Evaluation Metrics for ANN

Learning Algorithm	Evaluation Metrics					
	Accuracy	Precision	Recall	F1 Score	ROC-AUC	Training Time (s)
ANN	0.9997	0.9995	1.0000	0.9997	0.9997	23.64

As shown in Table 4.4, the comparison of the effectiveness of various metrics on ANN, the highest recall value of 1.0000 out of all the metrics, while Precision gave the lowest value of 0.99995. A training time of 23.64s was used to build the model.

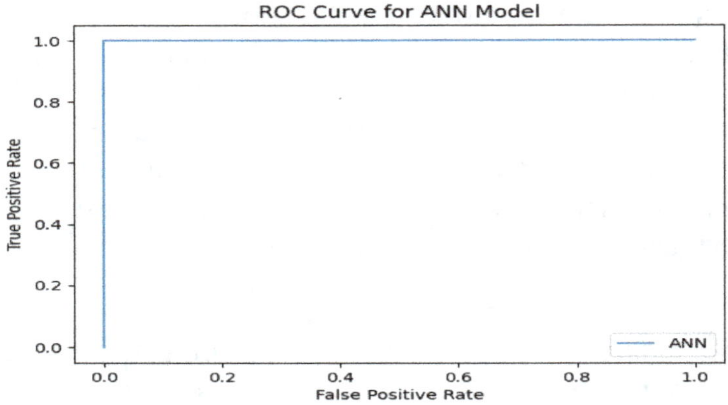

Figure 4.4: ROC-AUC curve for ANN

The ROC curve displayed for the ANN classifier demonstrates exceptional classification performance. Similar to the KNN model, the ANN's ROC curve rises sharply to the top-left corner (True Positive Rate = 1.0, False Positive Rate = 0.0). This indicates that the ANN is capable of distinguishing between positive and negative classes with perfect accuracy.

The Area Under the Curve (AUC) for this model is very close to 1.0, confirming its outstanding performance in classifying the data. Therefore, the ANN classifier appears to have no errors in classification, i.e., no false positives or false negatives.

Both KNN and ANN produced nearly identical perfect ROC curves. This might be a reflection of the dataset rather than the classifiers' unique strengths. ANN models generally perform well on complex, nonlinear problems, so further evaluation might be necessary to understand if this success stems from dataset simplicity or model sophistication.

4.5 Results of the Ensemble Approach (Bagging)

Table 4.5: Evaluation Metrics for Bagging (Voting) Classifier

Learning Algorithm	Evaluation Metrics					
	Accuracy	Precision	Recall	F1 Score	ROC-AUC	Training Time (s)
Bagging Classifier	0.9996	0.9993	0.9998	0.9996	0.9996	27.59

As shown in Table 4.5, the comparison of the various metrics effectiveness on the Bagging Classifier was conducted. The evaluation metrics of the developed botnet detection model using the Bagging (Voting) classifier demonstrate exceptional performance across all criteria. With an accuracy of 99.96%, the model exhibits an outstanding ability to correctly classify botnet and non-botnet traffic.

The precision of 99.93% indicates an extremely low false positive rate, meaning the model reliably predicts botnet activities without mislabelling benign traffic. Furthermore, the recall of 99.98% ensures that the model effectively detects nearly all botnet activities, minimizing the risk of false negatives. The F1-score of 99.96% reflects a balanced trade-off between precision and recall, affirming the robustness of the model in handling both classes.

The ROC-AUC score of 99.96% confirms the model's

excellent capability to distinguish between botnet and benign traffic across various decision thresholds. Additionally, the training time of only 27.59 seconds highlights the efficiency of the Bagging classifier, making it suitable for real-world applications where both accuracy and computational efficiency are critical. Therefore, the results indicate that the model is highly effective, scalable, and reliable for botnet detection in IoT environments.

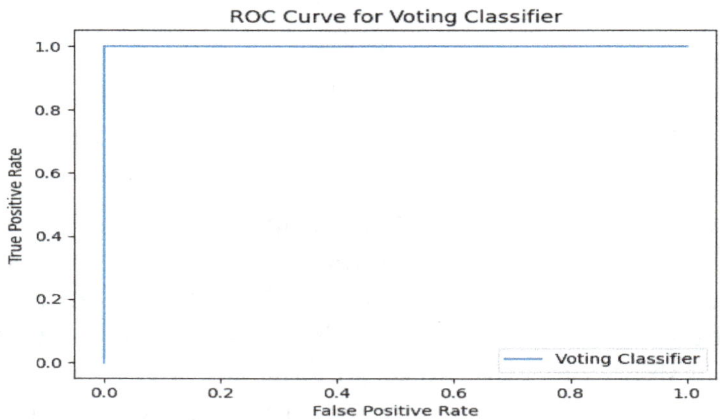

Figure 4.5: ROC-AUC curve for Bagging Classifier

4.6 Comparison of Performance Metrics for Base and Ensemble Classifiers

Table 4.6 compares the performance metrics, expressed in percentage, and training times of the 5 models: Linear Regression, Logistic Regression, KNN, ANN and Bagging (Voting) classifier.

Table 4.6: Comparison of Performance Metrics of Learners

Learning Algorithm	Evaluation Metrics					
	Accuracy	Precision	Recall	F1 Score	ROC-AUC	Training Time (s)
Linear Regression	91.37%	99.39%	83.26%	90.61%	91.37%	0.43
Logistic Regression	99.88%	99.85%	99.91%	99.88%	99.88%	3.34
KNN	99.98%	99.97%	99.99%	99.98%	99.98%	0.13
ANN	99.98%	99.96%	100.00%	99.98%	99.98%	23.64
Bagging Classifier	99.96%	99.93%	99.98%	99.96%	99.96%	27.59

The results displayed in Table 4.6 compare the performance of the five machine learning algorithms, Linear Regression, Logistic Regression, KNN, ANN, and Bagging Classifier, on the botnet attack detection task.

Linear Regression shows significantly lower performance compared to the other models, with an accuracy of 91.37%, a recall of 83.26%, and an F1-score of 90.61%. Despite having a high precision (99.39%), its recall is inadequate, suggesting it struggles to detect botnet activities effectively. Its ROC-AUC score of 91.37% also indicates relatively weak classification capabilities. However, its training time of 0.43 seconds is very efficient.

Logistic Regression delivers much better results, achieving an accuracy, precision, recall, F1-score, and ROC-AUC of approximately 99.88%. This indicates strong performance across all evaluation metrics, with a training time of 3.34 seconds, making it both accurate and relatively fast.

KNN and ANN outperform Logistic Regression with near-perfect scores for all metrics. Both models achieve 99.98% accuracy, 99.99% recall, and 99.98% ROC-AUC, showcasing excellent detection capabilities. However, KNN is computationally more efficient, with a training time of only 0.13 seconds, compared to ANN's 23.64 seconds, indicating that KNN is more suitable for scenarios requiring rapid deployment.

The Bagging Classifier also demonstrates exceptional performance, with slightly lower metrics compared to KNN and ANN but still maintaining high accuracy (99.96%), precision (99.93%), recall (99.98%), and ROC-AUC (99.96%). Its training time of 27.59 seconds is higher, making it less efficient than KNN but potentially more robust due to ensemble learning.

While KNN and ANN show the best detection performance, KNN stands out for its computational efficiency, and Bagging offers a good balance between performance and robustness. Linear Regression lags significantly and may not be suitable for this use case.

4.7 Performance Evaluation of Existing Studies

In this section, the results of the research are compared with the results obtained by some of the previous studies that were reviewed in the literature. Summary 4.7 shows that the results of the proposed model are better than the results obtained from the previous studies.

Summary 4.7: Overview of Results Compared to Previous Studies

S/No: 1

Author(s): Ali et al., 2024

Title: Hybrid Machine Learning Model for Efficient Botnet Attack Detection in IoT Environment.

Research Gap: An innovative botnet identification system, ACLR, which combined ANN, CNN, LSTM and RNN.

Methodology: Model stacking is employed. It combines the outputs of various deep learning algorithms ANN, CNN, LSTM, and RNN for final prediction.

Results: The ACLR model showed better performance than all other deep learning models with an accuracy score of 0.9698. ANN showed the poorest performance with an accuracy score of 0.7568.

S/No: 2

Author(s): Thota & Menaka, 2024

Title: Botnet detection in the internet-of-things networks using a convolutional neural network with a pelican optimization algorithm

Research Gap: Addressing the problem of severely imbalanced network traffic data in the training sets used for botnet attack detection in IoT networks.

Methodology: Designing and optimizing a Convolutional Neural Network (CNN) with a Pelican Optimization

Algorithm (POA) to detect botnet attacks in IoT networks.

Results: The proposed CNN-POA outperformed other existing metaheuristic algorithms (LGBA-NN, SDN, BMM and BiLSTM-CNN) with 99.5% accuracy.

S/No: 3

Author(s): Wardana et al., 2024

Title: Ensemble averaging deep neural network for botnet detection in heterogeneous Internet of Things devices.

Research Gap: Detecting botnet attacks within heterogeneous IoT devices.

Methodology: Development and training of individual DNN models. After training, the prediction outputs from each device-specific DNN model were aggregated. This aggregation was done using the ensemble averaging method.

Results: The ensemble-averaged DNN achieved an average accuracy of 97.21%, precision of 91.41%, recall of 87.31%, and an F1-score of 88.48%.

S/No: 4

Author(s): Mishra, Paliwal and Srivastava (2024)

Title: Anomaly detection using deep convolutional generative adversarial networks in the Internet of things.

Research Gap: A weighted stacked ensemble model that merges deep convolutional generative adversarial networks with Bi-LSTM networks.

Methodology: Employing an ensemble of neural networks for intrusion detection, utilizing datasets BOT-IoT, IoT-23, UNSWNB15, and ToN-IoT. BOT-IoT dataset This dataset captured various types of attacks for real-time analysis within the proposed framework.

Results: The model achieved a reduction in generalization error by 0.005%. It attained an exceptional accuracy of 99.99% for BOT-IoT, 99.08% for IoT23, 99.82% for UNSWNB15, and 99.96% for ToN_IoT datasets, accompanied by improvements in Precision, Recall, and F1-score.

S/No: 5

Author(s): Aremu Bolakale Lawal (2024)

Title: Botnet attack detection in the Internet of Things using selected learning algorithms (this work).

Research Gap: An ensemble machine learning model (Bagging) is developed using PCA, Linear Regression, Logistic Regression, KNN and ANN.

Methodology: The following machine learning models were trained and evaluated on the NB-IoT-23 datasets: Linear Regression, Logistic Regression, K-nearest neighbours (KNN), Artificial Neural Networks (ANN), and Bagging Classifier (Proposed Model).

Results: The model attained the following exceptional results:

- Accuracy: 99.96%
- Precision: 99.93%
- Recall: 99.98%
- F1 Score: 99.96%
- ROC-AUC: 99.96%
- Training Time: 27.59s

Summary 4.7 shows that this research presents significant advancements in botnet attack detection for IoT networks compared to the other studies reviewed. This research stands out for its exceptional results across all evaluation metrics, including an accuracy of 99.96%, precision of 99.93%, recall of 99.98%, F1-score of 99.96%, and an ROC-AUC of 99.96%. These metrics surpass the performance of the other existing methodologies, establishing the model as a highly reliable and efficient approach for botnet detection.

One key aspect that distinguishes this study is the balanced trade-off between performance and computational efficiency. While achieving near-perfect classification metrics, the model also maintains a reasonable training time of 27.59 seconds, highlighting its suitability for real-world deployment. This contrasts with methods like Wardana et al. (2024), whose ensemble-averaged DNN achieved an accuracy of 97.21% but showed significantly lower precision (91.41%), recall (87.31%), and F1-score (88.48%). Similarly, Ali et al. (2024)'s ACLR model reached only 96.98% accuracy, demonstrating inferior performance compared to the Bagging Classifier used in this research.

Moreover, Thota and Menaka (2024)'s CNN-POA model attained 99.5% accuracy, which is impressive but still falls short of the results obtained in this research in terms of comprehensive evaluation metrics. While Mishra, Paliwal and Srivastava (2024) achieved remarkable results with an accuracy of 99.99% on the BOT-IoT dataset, their model's generalizability across other datasets varied, with lower performance on IoT-23 and UNSWNB15 datasets (99.08% and 99.82%, respectively). In contrast, the approach of this research demonstrates consistent superiority using the NB-IoT-23 dataset, underlining its robustness in a realistic IoT environment.

Additionally, in this research, the use of dimensionality reduction through PCA and integration of both simple and complex algorithms (Linear Regression, Logistic Regression, KNN, ANN, and Bagging) makes the methodology more versatile and computationally efficient. This approach is unique compared to deep learning-heavy methods like ACLR and CNN-POA, which often require significantly more computational resources and time.

Therefore, this research stands out and is recommended for botnet attack detection because it combines high accuracy, efficiency, and robustness. It addresses a gap in previous studies by offering a scalable, reliable, and well-optimized model for detecting botnet attacks in IoT environments.

CHAPTER FIVE

SUMMARY, CONCLUSION AND RECOMMENDATION

5.1 Summary

This study presented a comprehensive analysis and evaluation of various machine-learning techniques for detecting botnet attacks in the Internet of Things (IoT) environment. Following an extensive review of existing methodologies, key shortcomings were identified in the approaches previously used, particularly concerning their adaptability to different IoT scenarios and datasets. To address these issues, four learners (Linear Regression, Logistic Regression, KNN and ANN) were trained and evaluated, using PCA for dimensionality reduction of the NB-IoT-23 datasets. These datasets encompassed a range of IoT devices targeted by the Gafgyt and Mirai botnets.

The learners were then ensembled to build a powerful Bagging Classifier of very high accuracy. The results obtained in this research demonstrate the effectiveness of the ensemble learning technique which is the Bagging approach, in detecting botnet attacks within IoT environments. The Bagging model achieved an accuracy of 99.96%, precision of 99.93%, recall of 99.98%, F1 score of 99.96%, and a ROC-AUC score of 99.96%, with a training time of 27.59 seconds.

5.2 Conclusion

These experimental results confirmed that:

i. PCA is reliable and acceptable for dimensionality reduction when using large NB-IoT-23 datasets, for training a machine learning model

ii. The bagging classifier is very effective and reliable for predicting botnet attacks because it achieves better results than some of the other models reviewed in the literature.

5.3 Contribution to Knowledge

The model's high accuracy and low computational overhead make it a viable solution for real-world applications of Botnet detection, contributing significantly to the ongoing efforts of stakeholders in securing IoT networks against botnet threats.

5.4 Recommendation

While this research has demonstrated the effectiveness of the Bagging model in detecting botnet attacks in IoT environments, there are several other exciting directions that future researchers can explore to build on these findings:

(i) Exploring New Datasets: Although the NB-IoT-23 datasets provided a solid foundation for this study, testing the Bagging model on other datasets that include a broader range of IoT devices and different types of botnets could be a valuable next step. This would help determine how well the model adapts to diverse real-world scenarios.

(ii) Real-Time Detection: Moving the Bagging model from the research setting into a real-time intrusion detection system (IDS) could make a big impact. Future researchers could focus on tweaking the model to ensure it works efficiently in real-time, especially in large, complex IoT networks where speed and scalability are crucial.

(iii) Comparing with Deep Learning Models: While this study focused on traditional machine learning techniques like ANN and KNN, it would be interesting to see how the Bagging model stacks up against more advanced deep learning models such as CNNs and RNNs. Exploring this could reveal important insights into the balance between accuracy, complexity, and computational needs.

(iv) Adaptive Learning for Evolving Threats: IoT environments are constantly changing, with new types of attacks different from Mirai and Gafgyt botnets, emerging all the time. Future research could focus on developing adaptive learning techniques that allow the model to continuously learn from new data, ensuring it stays effective against the latest threats.

(v) Balancing Privacy and Security: As machine learning models become more integrated into IoT networks, ensuring that they operate in a way that respects user privacy and data security is essential. Future researchers could explore ways to protect sensitive data while maintaining the high detection accuracy seen in this study.

(vi) Energy Efficiency: Many IoT devices have limited resources, so finding ways to make the Bagging model more energy-efficient would be a worthwhile challenge. Techniques like model pruning, compression, or using lighter algorithms could be explored to keep the model's performance strong while reducing its energy demands.

By exploring these areas, future research can build on the successes of this study, contributing to the ongoing effort to make IoT networks safer and more secure against the ever-evolving threat of botnets.

5.5 How to Get Further Help & Support

If you need to have the code used to get the results described in this research, or if you simply need more help in any area of your research, please feel free to reach out to me using the support email address provided below. I will respond within 12 hours or sooner.

Cheers,

Bolakale Aremu (CEO and Primary Author of this research)

AB Publisher LLC

ABPublisherLLC@gmail.com

https://leanpub.com/u/ablawal

REFERENCES

Abosata, N., Al-Rubaye, S., Inalhan, G., & Emmanouilidis, C. (2021, June 1). Internet of Things for system integrity: A comprehensive survey on security, attacks and countermeasures for industrial applications. *Sensors*. MDPI AG. Retrieved from https://doi.org/10.3390/s21113654

Adeniyi, & Oyelakin. (2023). A SURVEY ON PROMISING DATASETS AND RECENT MACHINE LEARNING APPROACHES FOR THE CLASSIFICATION OF ATTACKS IN THE INTERNET OF THINGS. *Journal of Information Technology and Computing*, 4(2), 31–38. Retrieved 12 April 2024 from https://doi.org/10.48185/JITC.V4I2.890

Alaiz-Moreton, H., Aveleira-Mata, J., Ondicol-Garcia, J., Muñoz-Castañeda, A. L., García, I., & Benavides, C. (2019). Multiclass Classification Procedure for Detecting Attacks on MQTT-IoT Protocol. *Complexity*, 2019. Retrieved 7 April 2024 from https://doi.org/10.1155/2019/6516253

Ali, M., Shahroz, M., Mushtaq, M. F., Alfarhood, S., Safran, M., & Ashraf, I. (2024). Hybrid Machine Learning Model for Efficient Botnet Attack Detection in IoT Environment. *IEEE Access*, 12, 40682–40699. Retrieved 1 May 2024 from https://doi.org/10.1109/ACCESS.2024.3376400

Aral, R. A., Keskin, S. R., Kaya, M., & Haciömeroğlu, M. (2018). Classification of TrashNet Dataset Based on Deep Learning Models. *Proceedings - 2018 IEEE International Conference on Big Data, Big Data 2018*, 2058–2062. Retrieved 19 April 2024 from https://doi.org/10.1109/BIGDATA.2018.8622212

Arnold, C., & Voigt, K. I. (2019). Determinants of Industrial Internet of Things Adoption in German Manufacturing Companies. *Https://Doi.Org/10.1142/S021987701950038X*, 16(6). Retrieved 7 April 2024 from https://doi.org/10.1142/S021987701950038X

Dang, N. C., Moreno-García, M. N., & De la Prieta, F. (2020). Sentiment Analysis Based on Deep Learning: A Comparative Study. *Electronics 2020, Vol. 9, Page 483*, 9(3), 483. Retrieved 19 April 2024 from https://doi.org/10.3390/ELECTRONICS9030483

Dange, S., & Chatterjee, M. (2020). IoT Botnet: The Largest Threat to the IoT Network. *Advances in Intelligent Systems and Computing*, 1049, 137–157. Retrieved 7 April 2024 from https://doi.org/10.1007/978-981-15-0132-6_10

Diro, A. A., & Chilamkurti, N. (2018). Distributed attack detection scheme using deep learning approach for Internet of Things. *Future Generation Computer Systems*, 82, 761–768. Retrieved 20 April 2024 from https://doi.org/10.1016/J.FUTURE.2017.08.043

Farzaneh, B., Koosha, M., Boochanpour, E., & Alizadeh, E. (2020a). A New Method for Intrusion Detection on RPL Routing Protocol Using Fuzzy Logic. *2020 6th International Conference on Web Research, ICWR 2020*, 245–250. Retrieved 6 April 2024 from https://doi.org/10.1109/ICWR49608.2020.9122278

Farzaneh, B., Koosha, M., Boochanpour, E., & Alizadeh, E. (2020b). A New Method for Intrusion Detection on RPL

Routing Protocol Using Fuzzy Logic. *2020 6th International Conference on Web Research, ICWR 2020*, 245–250. Retrieved 7 April 2024 from https://doi.org/10.1109/ICWR49608.2020.9122278

Ferrag, M. A., Maglaras, L., Moschoyiannis, S., & Janicke, H. (2020). Deep learning for cyber security intrusion detection: Approaches, datasets, and comparative study. *Journal of Information Security and Applications*, 50, 102419. Retrieved 20 April 2024 from https://doi.org/10.1016/J.JISA.2019.102419

Gandhi, R., & Li, Y. (2021). Comparing Machine Learning and Deep Learning for IoT Botnet Detection. *Proceedings - 2021 IEEE International Conference on Smart Computing, SMARTCOMP 2021*, 234–239. Retrieved 20 April 2024 from https://doi.org/10.1109/SMARTCOMP52413.2021.00053

Haner, J. K., & Knake, R. K. (2021). Breaking botnets: A quantitative analysis of individual, technical, isolationist, and multilateral approaches to cybersecurity. *Journal of Cybersecurity*, 7(1). Retrieved from https://doi.org/10.1093/cybsec/tyab003

Luthra, S., Garg, D., Mangla, S. K., & Singh Berwal, Y. P. (2018). Analyzing challenges to Internet of Things (IoT) adoption and diffusion: An Indian context. In *Procedia Computer Science* (Vol. 125, pp. 733–739). Elsevier B.V. Retrieved from https://doi.org/10.1016/j.procs.2017.12.094

Mahesh, B. (2018). Machine Learning Algorithms-A Review. *International Journal of Science and Research*.

Retrieved from https://doi.org/10.21275/ART20203995

Marshan, A., Nizar, F. N. M., Ioannou, A., & Spanaki, K. (2023). Comparing Machine Learning and Deep Learning Techniques for Text Analytics: Detecting the Severity of Hate Comments Online. *Information Systems Frontiers*, 1, 1–19. Retrieved 21 April 2024 from https://doi.org/10.1007/S10796-023-10446-X/FIGURES/18

Mashaleh, A. S., Ibrahim, N. F. B., Alauthman, M., Almseidin, M., & Gawanmeh, A. (2024). IoT Smart Devices Risk Assessment Model Using Fuzzy Logic and PSO. *Computers, Materials & Continua*, 78(2), 2245–2267. Retrieved from https://doi.org/10.32604/cmc.2023.047323

McDermott, C. D., Majdani, F., & Petrovski, A. V. (2018). Botnet Detection in the Internet of Things using Deep Learning Approaches. *Proceedings of the International Joint Conference on Neural Networks*, 2018-July. Retrieved 19 April 2024 from https://doi.org/10.1109/IJCNN.2018.8489489

Meidan, Y., Bohadana, M., Mathov, Y., Mirsky, Y., Shabtai, A., Breitenbacher, D., & Elovici, Y. (2018). N-BaIoT-Network-based detection of IoT botnet attacks using deep autoencoders. *IEEE Pervasive Computing*, 17(3), 12–22. Retrieved 11 April 2024 from https://doi.org/10.1109/MPRV.2018.03367731

Mishra, A. K., Paliwal, S., & Srivastava, G. (2024). Anomaly detection using deep convolutional generative adversarial networks in the Internet of things. *ISA Transactions*, 145, 493–504. Retrieved 1 May 2024 from https://doi.org/10.1016/J.ISATRA.2023.12.005

Pan, X., & Yamaguchi, S. (2022). Machine Learning White-Hat Worm Launcher for Tactical Response by Zoning in Botnet Defense System. *Sensors 2022, Vol. 22, Page 4666*, 22(13), 4666. Retrieved 7 April 2024 from https://doi.org/10.3390/S22134666

Roy, A., Qureshi, S., Pande, K., Nair, D., Gairola, K., Jain, P., ... Kakarlapudi, A. V. (2019). Performance Comparison of Machine Learning Platforms. *INFORMS Journal on Computing 31(2):207-225*, 31(2), 207–225. Retrieved 16 April 2024 from https://doi.org/10.1287/IJOC.2018.0825

Sai Kiran, K. V. V. N. L., Devisetty, R. N. K., Kalyan, N. P., Mukundini, K., & Karthi, R. (2020). Building an Intrusion Detection System for IoT Environment using Machine Learning Techniques. In *Procedia Computer Science* (Vol. 171, pp. 2372–2379). Elsevier B.V. Retrieved from https://doi.org/10.1016/j.procs.2020.04.257

Sharma, A., Mansotra, Prof. V., & Singh, K. (2023). Detection of Mirai Botnet Attacks on IoT Devices Using Deep Learning. *Journal of Scientific Research and Technology*, 174–187. Retrieved 3 May 2024 from https://doi.org/10.5281/ZENODO.8330561

Shwartz-Ziv, R., & Armon, A. (2022). Tabular data: Deep learning is not all you need. *Information Fusion*, 81, 84–90. Retrieved 19 April 2024 from https://doi.org/10.1016/J.INFFUS.2021.11.011

Son, & Mohammed. (2011). *4 Advanced Methods for Botnet Intrusion Detection Systems*. Retrieved from www.intechopen.com

Srivastava, V., Debnath, S. K., Stănică, P., & Pal, S. K. (2023). Multivariate identity-based broadcast encryption with applications to the Internet of things. *Advances in Mathematics of Communications*, 17(6), 1302–1313. Retrieved 6 May 2024 from https://doi.org/10.3934/AMC.2021050

Thota, S., & Menaka, D. (2024). Botnet detection in the internet-of-things networks using a convolutional neural network with the Pelican optimization algorithm. *Automatika*, 65(1), 250–260. Retrieved 3 May 2024 from https://doi.org/10.1080/00051144.2023.2288486

Truby, J. (2018, October 1). Decarbonizing Bitcoin: Law and policy choices for reducing the energy consumption of Blockchain technologies and digital currencies. *Energy Research and Social Science*. Elsevier Ltd. Retrieved from https://doi.org/10.1016/j.erss.2018.06.009

Ullah, I., & Mahmoud, Q. H. (2020). A two-level flow-based anomalous activity detection system for IoT networks. *Electronics (Switzerland)*, 9(3). Retrieved from https://doi.org/10.3390/electronics9030530

Wahida, U., #1, B., Sofiah, W. I., Din, W., Prasetyo, Y. A., Musa, Z., & Kasim, S. (2018). Internet of Things: An Implementation and Its Challenges in Malaysia, 8(6).

Wang, P., Fan, E., & Wang, P. (2021). Comparative analysis of image classification algorithms based on traditional machine learning and deep learning. *Pattern Recognition Letters*, 141, 61–67. Retrieved 19 April 2024 from https://doi.org/10.1016/J.PATREC.2020.07.042

Wardana, A. A., Kołaczek, G., Warzyński, A., & Sukarno,

P. (2024). Ensemble averaging deep neural network for botnet detection in heterogeneous Internet of Things devices. *Scientific Reports*, 14(1). Retrieved 3 May 2024 from https://doi.org/10.1038/S41598-024-54438-6

Wazzan, M., Algazzawi, D., Bamasaq, O., Albeshri, A., & Cheng, L. (2021, June 2). Internet of Things botnet detection approaches: Analysis and recommendations for future research. *Applied Sciences (Switzerland)*. MDPI AG. Retrieved from https://doi.org/10.3390/app11125713

Winkler, I., Gomes, A. T., & Shackleford, D. (2017). Advanced persistent security : a cyberwarfare approach to implementing adaptive enterprise protection, detection, and reaction strategies. *Published in **2017***. Retrieved 8 April 2024 from https://lib.ugent.be/catalog/ebk01:3710000000918309

Woodiss-Field, A., Johnstone, M. N., & Haskell-Dowland, P. (2024). Examination of Traditional Botnet Detection on IoT-Based Bots. *Sensors 2024, Vol. 24, Page 1027*, 24(3), 1027. Retrieved 3 May 2024 from https://doi.org/10.3390/S24031027

Wu, M., Lu, T. J., Ling, F. Y., Sun, J., & Du, H. Y. (2010). Research on the architecture of the Internet of Things. *ICACTE 2010 - 2010 3rd International Conference on Advanced Computer Theory and Engineering, Proceedings*, 5. Retrieved 7 April 2024 from https://doi.org/10.1109/ICACTE.2010.5579493